Scott Cohen's

FAMILY FRIENDLY
landscapes

backyards built for fun and games

Schiffer Publishing Ltd

4880 Lower Valley Road • Atglen, PA 19310

Other Schiffer Books by the Author:
Scott Cohen's Poolscapes:
Refreshing Ideas for the Ultimate Backyard Resort,
978-0-7643-3740-6, $39.99
Petscaping: Training and Landscaping with Your Pet in Mind,
978-0-7643-3854-0, $24.99

Other Schiffer Books on Related Subjects:
Pools, Patios, and Fabulous Outdoor Living Spaces, 0-7643-1994-9, $49.95
New Ideas for Living Outdoors, 978-0-7643-3533-4, $24.99

Library of Congress Control Number: 2012953137

Designed by Justin Watkinson
Type set in Chalet-LondonNineteenSeventy/Zurich BT

ISBN: 978-0-7643-4427-5
Printed in China

Published by Schiffer Publishing, Ltd.
4880 Lower Valley Road
Atglen, PA 19310
Phone: (610) 593-1777; Fax: (610) 593-2002
E-mail: Info@schifferbooks.com

For the largest selection of fine reference
books on this and related subjects,
please visit our website at:
www.schifferbooks.com.
You may also write for a free catalog.

This book may be purchased from the publisher.
Please try your bookstore first.

We are always looking for people to
write books on new and related subjects.
If you have an idea for a book,
please contact us at:
proposals@schifferbooks.com.

Schiffer Books are available at special discounts
for bulk purchases for sales promotions or premiums.
Special editions, including personalized covers,
corporate imprints, and excerpts can be created
in large quantities for special needs.
For more information contact the publisher.

In Europe, Schiffer books
are distributed by
Bushwood Books
6 Marksbury Ave.
Kew Gardens
Surrey TW9 4JF England
Phone: 44 (0) 20 8392 8585;
Fax: 44 (0) 20 8392 9876
E-mail: info@bushwoodbooks.co.uk
Website: www.bushwoodbooks.co.uk

Introduction: The Family that Plays Together   5

Chapter 1: Come Out and Play   6

Chapter 2: Kindergardening   12

Chapter 3: Get Your Game On   35

Chapter 4: Lawn Games and More   50

Chapter 5: Splash Happy Fun   67

Chapter 6: Entertaining with Ease   103

Afterword   128

Contents

Dedication

For my Mom and Dad,
who always made sure our yard
was the best place to be.

The Family that Plays Together...

When I was young, my parents always made sure our yard was the favorite hang-out for me and my friends. It was a completely comfortable spot where we could relax, play games, swim, talk, joke, flirt, and grow up together. My Dad and I built a large fourteen-foot treehouse complete with an eighty-foot-long zipline! Of course, I didn't know then that our fantastic backyard was part of Mom and Dad's strategy for keeping us close, safe, and under their supervision. However, it was also an important part of the glue that bonded our family together.

My wife, Lisa, and I have always shared my parents' philosophy about having our own backyard as "the place to be." We know that a comfortable, fun backyard is a family investment that pays off in countless ways.

As a garden designer and contractor, I've been building backyards for California families for twenty-five years and I've learned what works and what falls flat. I've discovered entertaining secrets that add life to backyard get-togethers, and I've learned to avoid common party design pitfalls.

In this book, I'll share my favorite ideas and tips with you. I hope they help you create a fun, playful, and entertaining backyard — one that keeps you outside long after the sun goes down and keeps your family together for years.

Scott Cohen

Introduction

CHAPTER 1

Come Out and Play

Basic Design Elements of a Family Friendly Backyard

Think of your yard as an extension of your home. Inside the house there are rooms where the whole family enjoys time together, but there are also rooms for entertaining guests and that give kids and adults space to do their own thing.

Your backyard can serve those same functions. It can be a place where you, your family, and guests all feel at home. It's a place where you can play with your kids and one that becomes their hang-out of choice during the tween and teen years. It's a place where grown-ups can have their own time too, where they can have plenty of rowdy juvenile entertainment — or not — as the mood dictates.

This is the family-friendly backyard — and it's a yard you'll always want to come home to.

A Ten-Year Window

Creating this kind of yard begins with a thoughtful plan. Whether you're considering a complete redesign or just a few upgrades, you'll want to plan a yard that can evolve with your changing family.

I like to use a ten-year window. What does your family need today and how will those needs change within ten years? A play-space designed for your three-year-old will look a lot different from a hang-out for pre-teens and teens. Your yard should easily flex and change as your kids grow.

If you're installing a gym set now, think about how you'll adapt it when the kids are done with teeter totters and swings. Is this a good spot for a bigger climbing wall, a fort, or a trampoline? The sandbox area that provides plenty of entertainment during the preschool and early elementary school years might also be the perfect spot for a hot tub later on. Look into the future and use your imagination.

In my own backyard, a sandbox became a play area and then when the kids outgrew the play set we converted the area into a Bocce ball court.

One of the author's daughters, above at nine months old and below at sixteen years old (in the foreground).

A Place of Their Own

Inside the house, adults and kids often have special spaces to call their own. Whether it's a bedroom, a playroom, or even a corner of the living room, kids enjoy having a spot that looks and feels like it belongs to them.

Ideally, especially if you have young children, your backyard will offer that same special place. It doesn't have to be big. Whether it's a full-sized playhouse with its own little yard, a sandy play area, or a small child's vegetable garden, the point is to offer kids a place where they can add their own special touch.

Whatever the size or scope, plan to decorate the area with the whimsical look that kids love. You may want to screen or partially screen the area with a trellis or garden wall. Not only does this give kids the privacy and fort-like feel they crave, it also offers an out-of-the-way place to stash the scooters, ride-on toys, and bubble mower before the adult guests arrive for cocktail hour.

A smooth garden wall provides privacy and makes a great chalkboard surface. Apply a smooth stucco coat and paint with primer. Then apply two coats of chalkboard paint. Give the kids a bucket of sidewalk chalk and watch them go to town.

▲ *The yard when it was set up for small children.*

▼ *As it looks today now that they are teenagers.*

Photo by Diedra Walpole.

Grown-Up Time

Adults need their space too. Be sure to include an outdoor living area you can design and decorate for your own relaxation. You might want to include a fireplace, a covered patio, a dining area, or other amenities to create an inviting ambiance conducive to grown-up conversation, reading, or romance.

Entertaining

As you build your plan, consider your entertaining needs for both kids and adults. Do you typically host only small get-togethers for two or three couples? Or do you want your yard to be the scene of big, multi-family barbecues? Are you designing a space for your own family getaway or will you also be hosting big birthday parties with thirty or forty kids plus a magician and twenty teens by the pool?

Design your yard for both everyday family comfort and easy entertaining. If you often host large groups with several families, plan for a separate space for active child's play so that games of Hide and Seek aren't tearing through the conversation area.

Game On

A family-friendly yard is one designed for outdoor fun. It's a yard that draws kids and adults away from video games and computers to play outside. Think about the games your family loves to play — or would play if they had the right space — and build that space into your yard design, whether it's a sport court, a putting green, a hopscotch path, or a stretch of lawn perfect for croquet or football.

Remember the Furry Family Members

Petscaping™ is a growing trend in landscape design. Simple details can make backyard living more fun for you and your dog. How about a stretch of lawn for a game of Frisbee or an agility course? Maybe install a small pond for an afternoon dog paddle? Don't forget that shady napping spot.

A family-friendly landscape is all in the details. In the following pages, you'll discover how to design all of these spaces and more. So take some time to start dreaming and making notes about your ideal "come-out-and-play" backyard. Then read on to find out how to bring those dreams to life.

CHAPTER 2
Kindergardening

Designing a Backyard for Children of Different Ages

For most parents, a safe, inviting place for kids to play outdoors is a top priority. A yard designed around the growing needs of the younger set will encourage children of all ages to get outside and play every chance they get. Whether you're a parent, grandparent, aunt, or uncle, here are some ways to create a yard that inspires hours of active play for your family and young visitors.

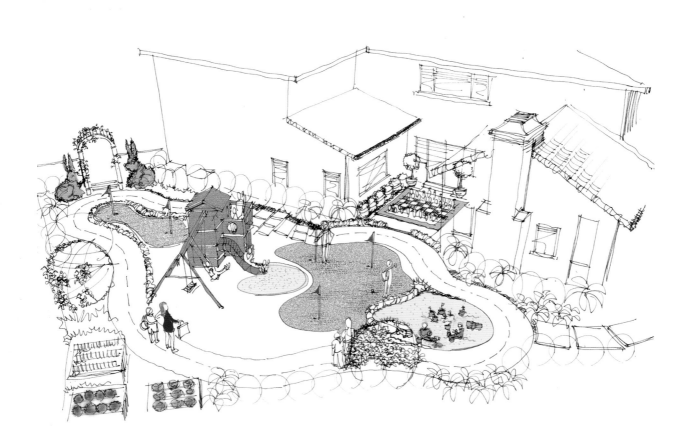

Play Set Design

If you have the space, a play set makes a great addition to any family-friendly yard. Swings, slides, and climbing equipment will keep kids entertained and help them burn all that energy (which means they'll be ready for bed when adults are ready for grown-up time).

However, don't underestimate the space you'll need. Most suppliers offer a plan showing the measurements required for the footprint of the equipment itself. In many cases, though, this isn't enough for comfort. Often overlooked is the additional elbow-room needed for swinging as high as possible, for jumping off mid-air, or for landing at the bottom of the slide and sprinting away without colliding into fences, walls, or unsuspecting guests.

Locate the play set apart from the main lawn area where it won't interrupt general traffic flow and lawn games. To avoid locking yourself into a regime of watering your swings and trimming around your slide, consider installing a soft, low maintenance material under and around the play set. Wood bark or recycled rubber mulch are suitable choices. *Note: If you have dogs, DO NOT use cocoa fiber mulch or cocoa shell mulch – they can be very toxic if ingested by dogs!*

Sand Play

Surrounding the play set with a large sandbox area is another low maintenance option. Sand makes for soft landings and offers endless possibilities for creative play. All that's required is a weed barrier base, the sand, and a way to contain it. Avoid using old railroad ties, which were heavily treated with pesticides and preservatives. There's no reason to expose kids to industrial chemicals (not to mention the slivers). Instead, consider faux ties from companies like Garden Ties. These are made from recycled materials and are sturdy enough to hold up to the kinds of abuse kids and the elements can dish out.

You can also personalize your sandbox and other areas of your yard with decorative borders. With a cast concrete curb, you can create a free-form shape for the sandbox and embellish it with stamped designs or letters. Some people stamp it with family names, handprints, or favorite sayings. These small details are a great way to reflect the unique personality of the family who plays there.

Scram!

If there are cats on your block, don't let them turn your clean sandbox into the neighborhood cat box. Keep them (and the deer) out with a Scarecrow sprinkler. This motion-activated sprinkler will chase "Mittens" away before she has a chance to find her special spot.

Scarecrow® sprinkler head by Contech Electronics.

Pathways to Fun

"Wayfinding" is the word landscape designers and architects use to describe the flow of people from once space to another and the paths that lead them there. In a family-friendly yard, these paths can serve multiple functions for both traffic flow and play.

Riding Paths

Consider adding wheel-friendly paths to allow kids to put miles on their scooters, trikes, bikes, mini motor cars, skates, and more. Riding paths spark lots of games that kids of varying ages (with different vehicles) can all play together. This even gives your kids a chance to hone their handling skills safely in the yard before you turn them loose on the streets.

Concrete is ideal, but decomposed granite can work too, depending on your riding toys. Riding paths work especially well along flower beds where they can be used to separate the garden from the lawn. Plan your pathways at two to three feet wide for riders and one-way foot traffic. For two-way foot traffic, widen pathways to four feet for kids and five feet for adults. When traffic slows down a bit, adults appreciate the path as they stroll through the yard or tend the garden.

Hopscotch

Why just walk from the patio to the play area when you could hopscotch along the way? We typically pour the hopscotch court out of concrete and let the kids draw in their own numbers, but you can also set decorative tiles or stamp in the numerals. Multi-functional treatments like this help families pack a lot of fun into a small space.

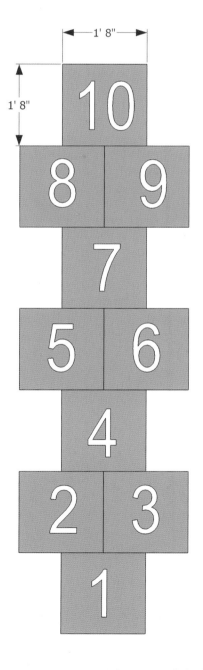

1' 8"

1' 8"

10

8 9

7

5 6

4

2 3

1

Design a hopscotch game into your garden pathway. A Hopscotch-playing board is made of ten 18"–24" squares. Get creative and use handmade tiles or specialty concrete stamp kits to number them.

Multi-Purpose Patios

Patios can serve multiple functions too. How about a Tic-tac-toe Patio? Or an outdoor living room that becomes an oversized chess or checker board on game night? Install large square pavers in two colors. Use Frisbees for oversized checkers. For added personality, monogram your Frisbee checkers with your family name or choose team names.

A Family that Gardens Together...

A garden can teach kids (and adults) a multitude of life lessons. Children of all ages appreciate the seemingly magic way the sun, soil, water, and seeds combine to produce food we can actually eat — and there's no better way to get your family to eat more fruits and vegetables than to turn the garden into a family project.

Fruit and vegetable gardening shows kids where some of our food supply comes from and helps them develop an appreciation for their role in environmental stewardship. A garden also gives kids a chance to develop the responsibility of caring for living things. It could even give them a chance to show Mom and Dad they're ready for a pet.

A garden is also just plain fun. It's a place where kids can get dirty and play in the mud without anyone telling them they're making a mess.

Easy Vegetables for Child's First Garden

CARROTS | RADISHES | POTATOES
PEAS | TOMATOES | PUMPKINS

Carrots are the classic starter vegetable for kids. They take up very little room and offer delicious rewards. Kids love to rake the carrot bed smooth with a hand rake. Leave a few spots lumpy and harvest all sorts of funny-shaped carrots later on.

CARROTS | **RADISHES** | POTATOES
PEAS | TOMATOES | PUMPKINS

Radishes germinate in a matter of days and mature quickly so they're perfect for eager young gardeners. Their crunchy spiciness is an interesting taste for developing palates.

CARROTS | RADISHES | **POTATOES**
PEAS | TOMATOES | PUMPKINS

Potatoes are super easy to grow. Kids love "digging for buried treasure" at harvest time.

CARROTS | RADISHES | POTATOES
PEAS | **TOMATOES** | PUMPKINS

Cherry or grape tomatoes offer another sweet treat kids can snack on right from the vine. Red, yellow, and orange varieties are available for colorful fun.

CARROTS | RADISHES | POTATOES
PEAS | TOMATOES | PUMPKINS

Snow and snap peas mature quickly. Kids love to snap them right off the vine and pop them in their mouths.

CARROTS | RADISHES | POTATOES
PEAS | TOMATOES | **PUMPKINS**

While they may take up more room, it's a lot of fun for kids to grow a pumpkin or two. For a humorous twist, kids can carve their initials, a face, or designs about 1/8" deep into a few small pumpkins early in the season. As the pumpkins grow, the designs will too.

GOOD ENOUGH TO EAT: Edible landscaping is a growing trend in garden design. Many food-bearing plants and trees can also serve nicely as ornamentals. Instead of confining them to the food garden, consider integrating them into beds or planter boxes throughout the landscape. My favorite ornamental and edible trees include oranges, lemons, limes, pomegranates, and plums.

Safe, Accessible, Fun

With a small lot and a large family, including a special needs child who uses a wheelchair, these clients wanted a yard that didn't limit access to fun. We created an environment that invites kids of all abilities to play together and where adults can relax and supervise in comfort. The yard includes a riding path suitable for both bikes and wheelchairs, along with a special trampoline that sits flush with the ground on one side. This allows the wheelchair to pull directly onto the edge of the trampoline and gives the child access to the trampoline without any climbing or lifting. Trampolines provide great exercise and help develop balance skills. This also solved the issue of this small yard's challenging grade variation. Dropping the front grade down eighteen inches while raising the grade in back brought the ground to the level we needed. Bench seating on one side gives kids a comfortable place to wait their turn. When the trampoline isn't in use, a small opening leads to a cozy "kids only" space underneath. The yard also features an outdoor kitchen and barbeque counter, a covered patio with seat walls, and a wishing well fountain.

Outdoor Recreation 101

With a recently completed pool, these clients were ready to finish their yard with features dedicated to all-out family fun. The existing pool already featured a beach entry, climbing rocks, and a slide. We finished the yard with a number of recreation stations that keep the action going in and out of the pool. Bocce ball players can compete on the 12' x 60' bocce court. In the side yard, a play area and sandbox bordered by a chalkboard retaining wall accommodates the family's play set. With a half-court basketball court and a putting green, the family won't outgrow this yard anytime soon.

Capture the Heat

Players would never know it as they're shooting baskets, but the entire basketball court is one big passive solar pool heating system. Serving as a thermal mass, the concrete soaks up the sun's heat during the day and retains it well into the evening. Piping circulates cool water from the pool through the concrete where it is warmed and sent back to the swimmers.

CHAPTER 2 Kindergardening

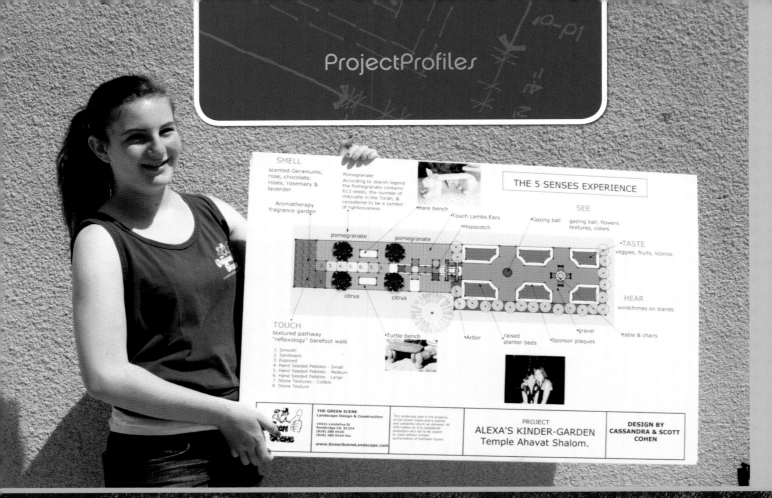

SMELL
scented Geraniums, rose, chocolate. roses, rosemary & lavender.

Aromatherapy fragrance garden

Pomegranate
According to Jewish legend the Pomegranate contains 613 seeds, the number of mitzvahs in the Torah, & considered to be a symbol of righteousness.

•Hare bench

•Touch Lambs Ears

•Hopscotch

pomegranate   pomegranate

citrus   citrus

TOUCH
textured pathway "reflexology" barefoot walk

1. Smooth
2. Sandwash
3. Exposed
4. Hand Seeded Pebbles - Small
5. Hand Seeded Pebbles - Medium
6. Hand Seeded Pebbles - Large
7. Stone Textures - Cobble
8. Stone Texture

•Turtle bench

THE 5 SENSES EXPERIENCE

SEE

•Gazing ball   gazing ball, flowers textures, colors

•TASTE
veggies, fruits, licorice.

HEAR
windchimes on stands.

•Arbor   •raised planter beds   •Sponsor plaques   •gravel   •table & chairs

THE GREEN SCENE
Landscape Design & Construction
19431 Londelius St
Northridge CA. 91324
(818) 280 0420
(818) 280 0424 Fax
www.GreenSceneLandscape.com

This landscape plan is the property of the Green Scene and is loaned and subjects return on demand. All information on it is considered proprietary and not to be copied or used without written authorization of theGreen Scene.

PROJECT
ALEXA'S KINDER-GARDEN
Temple Ahavat Shalom.

DESIGN BY
CASSANDRA & SCOTT
COHEN

A Five *Senses* Kinder-Garden

Developed as my daughter Cassandra's Bat Mitzvah project in honor of Alexa Weiner, her childhood friend who passed away, this "Five-Senses Garden" has now become a colorful celebration of life. It required a team of enthusiastic volunteers to install and offered an excellent opportunity for several families to get together to create a gift for the entire community.

The garden features elements that give children a number of creative ways to experience the textures, smells, tastes, sights, and sounds of nature. It begins with a reflexology path that gives bare feet a fun way to explore the sense of touch. Reflexology is the ancient practice of applying various types of pressure to the foot to stimulate well-being. Little feet learn by walking along a path that transitions from smooth concrete to rough sand-wash to tickly pebbles to cool, round cobble. For another touchable experience, a bed of velvety lamb's ear is planted at the end of a colorful acid-stained hopscotch path.

This enchanting children's garden for a busy pre-school invites little ones to explore their world through a variety of engaging sensory experiences.

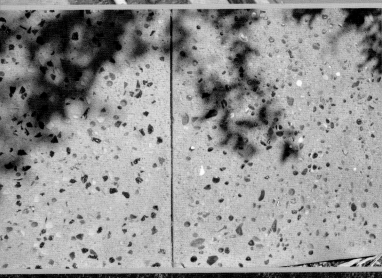

To create the reflexology path, we hand-seeded wet concrete with varying sized pebbles and recycled glass and then gently stamped them into the surface. As the concrete began to cure, we sponged the surface to expose the aggregates and glass. Each 2" x 2" square has a differently textured finish to stimulate little feet.

Middle school volunteers installed Marathon Dwarf Tall Fescue sod, selected for its hardiness for playgrounds. (LEFT, ABOVE, AND OPPOSITE PAGE)

To highlight the sense of smell, children experience a variety of delicious fragrances in an aromatherapy garden planted with rose and chocolate scented geraniums, roses, rosemary, lemon, nutmeg, and lavender.

Acid chemical stains are a great way to decoratively color plain gray concrete. The translucent acid stains create a rich, mottled, and textured look when applied with sponges. Acid stains actually burn into the concrete, making the improvements permanent. Volunteers wore thick gloves to protect their tender hands from the acid. Stains are available in a multitude of colors at your local masonry supply shop. For more creative decorative concrete ideas, visit www.ConcreteNetwork.com, one of the garden's sponsors.

Whimsical tortoise and hare benches from Phoenix Precast Products (www. phoenixprecastproducts. com) provide a playful touch and invite everyone to stop and smell the roses. Each bench is flanked by two small fruit trees. Pomegranates, clementines, and apples offer pick-and-eat treats. (ABOVE AND NEXT PAGE)

This type of dedication used in the Five Senses Garden for Alexa Weiner, called "Sentiments in Stone," can be special-ordered from Rinse Water Statuary (www.rwstatuary.com). To create the depth of the wording, text is applied with a stencil and then sandblasted into the concrete.

A wrought iron arbor adorned with Brazilian Butterfly Vine leads curious taste buds to raised planting beds on the other side of the garden. At harvest time, children can taste the vegetables, licorice, small fruits, and other edibles they've planted and tended themselves.

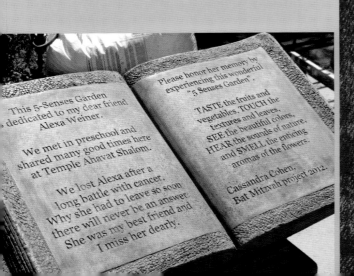

To stimulate the sense of sight, the garden features an abundance of colorful flowers, groundcovers, and shrubs in a variety of contrasting textures. A reflective gazing ball enhances the visual experience and raised vegetable planting beds were easily constructed using stackable pavers from AngelusBlock.com. Pavers were set with construction epoxy between courses of block. *(LEFT, ABOVE, AND OPPOSITE PAGE)*

The relaxing sounds of wind chimes ringing and leaves rustling in the breeze complete the five senses kinder-garden.

Hopscotch, Anyone?

It's easy to build a concrete hopscotch path. First, we placed sand and gravel as our base, then tied rebar steel reinforcement and cut our wood forms to size. Hopscotch pads are best sized at about 18" x 18". Once the concrete was brought in by wheelbarrow, we smoothed out the surface and tooled in our score joints. Later the concrete will be stained by volunteers.

CHAPTER 3

Get Your Game On

Designing and Installing Surfaces for Specific Sports

Think about the sports and hobbies you enjoy best — the ones that make you lose yourself for awhile or forget about coming in for dinner. With carefully chosen amenities, your yard can offer you and your family an opportunity to play some of these favorites more often. Here are some options and spacing guidelines to help you layout your own yard.

Hit the Court

C'mon, you know you want one! You may already have a basketball hoop out back, but if you're serious about your game, you can take it up a level. A simple surface coating can convert any concrete slab into an "official" game court for basketball or other sports.

Rubberized sport coatings are available in multiple colors. Applied with a trowel or squeegee, these high-performance surface treatments create a firm, textured game floor that offers just a bit of give for shock absorption underfoot. Whether your space accommodates the key, the three-point line, or a professional-sized half-court, a game surface with official markings lends an air of authenticity that's hard to resist.

Choose traditional green-on-green markings or personalize your court with your favorite team colors or a design that reflects your family. More subdued palettes can be used to create a court that blends in with the rest of the home and landscape, but no matter what colors you choose, game courts aren't just for team sports. Your court can continue to serve nicely as a patio or dance floor for entertaining and also works great for roller skating, biking, skateboarding, or any activity that calls for a smooth surface.

The kids wanted a basketball court, but in this smaller backyard, Mom didn't want it be overbearing so we used neutral colors on our coatings. The tan color background coordinates well with the hardscape and stonework in the rest of the yard. This play court doubles as patio space and a dance floor for larger parties.

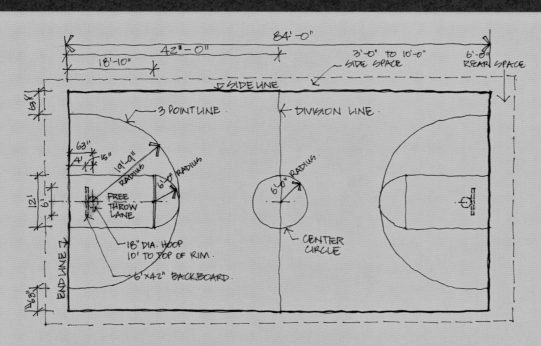

BASKETBALL COURT

* HIGH SCHOOL COURT SIZES.

84'-0"

42'-0"

18'-10"

3'-0" TO 10'-0" SIDE SPACE

6'-0" REAR SPACE

SIDELINE

3 POINT LINE

DIVISION LINE

63"

4'   15"

19'-9" RADIUS

6'-0" RADIUS

6'-0" RADIUS

FREE THROW LANE

18" DIA. HOOP
10' TO TOP OF RIM.

6'x42" BACKBOARD.

CENTER CIRCLE

ENDLINE

12'   6'

6'3"

Putting Practice

You don't have to be a serious golfer to get serious enjoyment out of a backyard putting green. Whether you want to shave points off your score or just have fun with the kids, a putting green outside your door offers a quick way to take a break and relax.

Be sure to consult a qualified installation contractor who can help you choose the right materials and design a green that will give you the type of golfing experience you're looking for. A green made for serious putting will require different specs than one designed for goofing around with the kids.

Faux turf greens are growing in popularity. They don't include the high maintenance headaches of real turf and they look nice year-round. Today's artificial turf is also much more authentic looking and performs better than it did in years' past.

Artificial turf putting greens can be set with varying heights of fringe. Sand, rubberized pellets, or other aggregates can provide fill to make the blades stand up, so you can achieve the surface performance you're looking for.

Extreme Sports

The clients for this property don't have kids, but as adults they easily maintain the high activity level and stamina of your average nine-year-old. They love their sports and they love the outdoors. They wanted a park-like setting where they (and their dogs) could find lots of ways to play together.

Their finished yard includes a pool with adjacent spa and waterslide, a trampoline, and a half-court basketball court. We created a center circle for the court featuring a basketball design that we custom-colored to produce a soft leather effect. When they're ready to cool down, the couple can enjoy their outdoor kitchen or relax by the fireplace in their outdoor living room.

Family Time

The kids in this family really enjoy basketball. The parents wanted to encourage this by adding a basketball court, but they didn't want the court to dominate the décor of this small yard. The parents also wanted to give their kids a chance to enjoy the kind of marshmallow roasts they remembered from their own childhoods.

Their remodeled yard includes a basketball court in neutral tan and brown earth tones that complement the rest of the landscape.

We remodeled the existing pool by adding bench seating around the perimeter, an oversized spa that comfortably accommodates the whole family, and a deep hydrotherapy well that's just big enough for two. (BELOW AND NEXT PAGE)

When it's time to warm up, the family can roast marshmallows and make memories around their poolside fire pit. The yard also features a large barbeque and a covered patio with a fire hearth.

Multi-Level Fun

After starting a second family together, this couple wanted a yard designed to entertain adults and young children. The client is an avid golfer with a property overlooking a golf course.

To take advantage of the property's view, we removed the existing lap pool and replaced it with a fan shaped vanishing edge pool and spa. With varying depths, the pool is safe for young children. A swim-up bar makes it just as easy to serve either cocktails or PBJ sandwiches at the pool. A pull-out hand-held spray jet in the spa adds to the fun.

This infinity edge pool and spa is veneered entirely in 1x1 mosaic glass tiles. The project received the prestigious Masters of Design award from pool and spa industry.

The beautiful new yard includes a 900-square-foot split-level putting green for the golfer and a large play area for the couple's young daughter. A new sandbox is bordered with pour-in-place cast concrete curbing. We stamped the concrete with her name and handprints while the pour was fresh.

MASTERS OF DESIGN®

hanley▲wood

Patio on the Green

Side yards are often a forgotten asset in landscape design. While they may be too small for large features, side yards usually offer valuable space that can be put to good use with a little creative thinking.

The clients for this yard are avid golfers. The space in their side yard offered enough room for us to add a golf-themed outdoor room and putting green. We created the golf-ball bistro patio using an oyster white color hardener. We chiseled off the color to form the dimples. We used a chemical stain to add the logo of the client's ball of choice. A decorative wood arbor delineates the space and a stamped concrete pathway leads from the backyard to this special room. (ABOVE AND NEXT TWO PAGES)

We also built a beautiful swimming pool for these clients with a raised spa and fire pit, and closer to the house, a covered dining pavilion and outdoor kitchen.

CHAPTER 4

Lawn Games and More

Making Space for Family Favorite Games

Bocce ball, shuffleboard, croquet, horseshoes — we all have our favorites. These are the casual lawn and court games made just for neighborhood cookouts, family reunions, and evenings at home with the kids. These are the fierce competitions that keep everyone laughing in the quest to determine who will be crowned the next Bocce Ball King or Ping Pong Princess.

The names change from one neighborhood to the next. "Ladderball" on one block might be "Blongo Ball" on another or "Hillbilly Golf" a few streets over. The rules change too. That's all part of the fun. (By the way, if you're playing at my house, you play by my rules — that's just how it works.)

Whatever the rules and whatever you call them, backyard games are a lot more fun if you have the right space to play them. Measure; don't guess. A few inches here or there can really make a difference. If you've ever tried playing ping-pong in a space that's too tight, you know exactly what I mean. Remember to include comfortable walk-

around space as well. Room for a couple of chairs for your cheering (or guffawing) fans is a nice perk too.

While all this planning might seem like overkill for casual backyard games, it really does pay off. The area you set up for your games might impact other landscape decisions too. Issues like drainage, irrigation, lighting, material selection, and tree placement all come into play (pun intended).

Your recreational equipment can often serve dual purposes. For example, during large parties, you can easily convert an outdoor ping-pong or pool table into an al fresco dining set with some chairs and a tablecloth.

A backyard designed for fun will make your home the hangout of choice as your kids grow from toddlers to teens. Most of all, it will give your whole family a place to relax, enjoy each other, and make memories. Here are space guidelines for some popular backyard games along with rules for a few of my favorites.

HORSESHOES | BOCCE BALL
LADDER BALL OR BLONGO BALL
SHUFFLEBOARD | TRAMPOLINES
VOLLEYBALL | TETHERBALL
"PING-PONG" OR TABLE TENNIS

Horseshoes can be played on lawn, gravel, decomposed granite, or sand. The standard play consists of two stakes forty feet apart; however, you can play with just one stake and draw a line at whatever distance you wish to play. Just make sure that you allow ample throw room. You wouldn't want to accidently hit any spectators. Rebound boards can be set behind each stake and built of 2-3 courses of rail ties or pressure treated lumber.

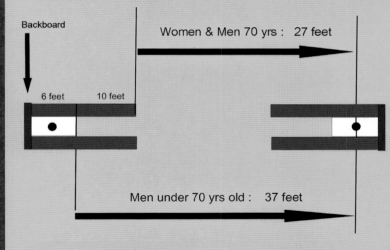

Backboard

Women & Men 70 yrs : 27 feet

6 feet   10 feet

Men under 70 yrs old :   37 feet

image courtesy of http://www.glenlakesfoleyal.com/

The standard size of a bocce ball court is 90 feet by 13 feet. However, you may construct one that is as short as 40 feet, depending on how seriously you take your Bocce. Proper drainage is critical to avoid water pooling in the court. Install French drains below ground using a perforated pipe, a canvas sleeve, and crushed gravel. Construct the perimeter game walls 6-18 inches high using rail ties, block, or cast concrete curbing to keep the balls on the playing field.

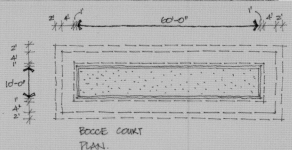

BOCCE COURT PLAN.

The popularity of this Old World Italian game is making a comeback in a big way. The long and narrow court surface should consist of a material that provides minimal bounce, such as decomposed granite, sand, or crushed oyster shell, none of which require any water.

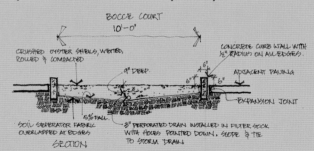

BOCCE COURT
10'-0"

CRUSHED OYSTER SHELLS, WETTED, ROLLED & COMPACTED
CONCRETE CURB WALL WITH ½" RADIUS ON ALL EDGES.
9" DEEP
ADJACENT PAVING
SOIL SEPERATOR FABRIC OVERLAPPED AT EDGES
5% FALL
3" PERFORATED DRAIN INSTALLED IN FILTER SOCK WITH HOLES POINTED DOWN. SLOPE & TIE TO STORM DRAIN
EXPANSION JOINT
SECTION

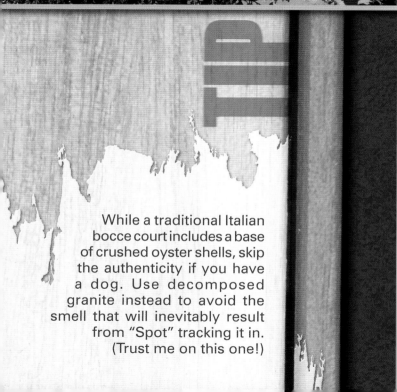

While a traditional Italian bocce court includes a base of crushed oyster shells, skip the authenticity if you have a dog. Use decomposed granite instead to avoid the smell that will inevitably result from "Spot" tracking it in. (Trust me on this one!)

This is a great party game for the whole family. You can play this on grass, sand, dirt, decomposed granite, or concrete. The game consists of two Blongo Goals with bars across them. Colorful pairs of golf balls are connected to each other with 12-18 inches of rope. Teams take turns tossing the roped golf balls across the court to wrap around the other players' goals. Officially, the rules call for the goals to stand 25 feet apart, but you can move them to any distance you want depending on the age and skill of your players. Typically the goals are constructed of PVC pipe so they are easily transportable.

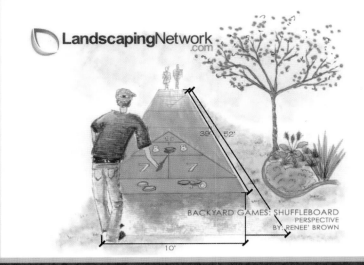

BACKYARD GAMES: SHUFFLEBOARD
PERSPECTIVE
BY: RENEE' BROWN

Shuffleboard is played on a court that is 6 feet wide by 39 feet long, with 6 feet x 6 inch standing room at either end. It should be on a flat surface that allows the discs to easily slide. You can pour a concrete slab and stain or paint the various sections of the court the appropriate colors.

Trampolines are loved by kids and adults of all ages. It's a great form of exercise and takes up little space in the yard. Trampolines vary in size from 8-14 feet in diameter. Lawns don't seem to survive well under trampolines, so plan an area with gravel or decomposed granite for long-term placement. The trampoline in this children's play yard was recessed down to accommodate wheelchair access for a special needs child.

CHAPTER 4 Lawn Games and More

A volleyball court consists of the playing area and the safety space around the boundary, which measures a total of 50 x 80 feet. Of course, you can make it smaller to accommodate your yard. You will need to excavate a 1.5- to 3-foot deep area and install a drainage ditch that leads water away from the lowest point of the court or install French style drains. Overlay the area with a one-foot thick layer of smooth gravel. Then install a layer of burlap or landscape fabric and place one to two feet of beach sand or washed masonry sand on top. Rake and level out the sand. (Note: While outdoor volleyball is commonly played on sand, you can also construct a playing area of clay or grass. Whatever your preference, it is important to make sure it has proper drainage and that the area above the court is an open space.)

Use a removable pole and almost any large patio can be converted into a tetherball court! Tetherball is played on a flat circle court about 20 feet in diameter with a 10- to 12-foot pole placed in the center. The circle can consist of concrete, sand, decomposed granite, or grass. It should be an area on which people can easily maneuver as they hit the ball back and forth.

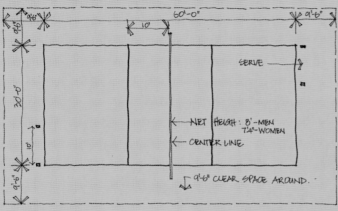

VOLLEYBALL COURT

HORSESHOES | BOCCE BALL
LADDER BALL OR BLONGO BALL
SHUFFLEBOARD | TRAMPOLINES
VOLLEYBALL | TETHERBALL
"PING-PONG" OR TABLE TENNIS

Table Tennis, or ping-pong, can be played outdoors with a table that is made specifically for outdoor use. The table size is 9 x 5 feet. You will want to place it on a flat surface, such as a concrete patio. The playing area should be about 28 x 14 feet to allow for players to move around. Of course, you may want to build the patio near a lawn area for those few times you may need to chase the ping-pong ball.

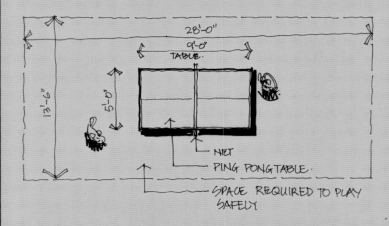

PING PONG

Plan and Measure

Draw up your plans carefully. Every game has its own required measurements. Sometimes only two or three feet make all the difference between an area that works for the games you want to play and one that doesn't quite make it.

Don't worry if you can't find room for everything. Set aside space for your favorites and design it well. Your yard will get much more use if you allow enough room for players to stretch out and move.

Often, one modestly sized area can serve multiple purposes. A paved pathway makes a great hopscotch court — especially when the pathway leads to the children's play space or playhouse. How about a Tic Tac Toe patio or a larger patio with pavers in two colors that makes an oversized checker/chess board? Use Frisbees in two colors for the checkers. You can order these online imprinted with your own family logo!

▲ One of my favorite indoor games is Scrabble. Look at what this couple did to improve their vocabulary and family fun together outdoors. Sacramento architect Kristy McAuliffe created this five-foot concrete game board. For more information, go to http://www.sunset.com/garden/backyard-projects/backyard-scrabble-00400000013845/. Photo by E. Spencer Toy.

▼ Order a giant chess set – like this one – from a store like GreatBigStuff.com and you're ready to turn this quiet parlor game for two into a lively outdoor team sport.

My family plays volleyball, badminton, and tetherball all on the same backyard lawn and we mark out the court dimensions using upside down spray chalk. The brightly colored chalk does not harm the grass in any way and is readily available at any hardware or home-improvement store.

When planning out your play areas, make sure to consider your lighting needs. Outdoor lighting will help keep the games going when the sun goes down.

A yard that grows with the family: Consider the long-range plans for your yard as your kids mature. Maybe the area you set aside for the playhouse today is the perfect size for the hot tub you're planning to install later.

Gaming Grounds

The owners of this backyard are mature adults who wanted a special place to entertain their visiting grandchildren. Their large lot is located in an arid part of the San Fernando Valley, so heat and drought tolerance were a concern.

We added several gaming areas, including a shuffleboard court, a putting green, and horseshoe pit. A covered patio for shade along with a pond and basalt stone fountain creates a cooling sanctuary from the intense afternoon heat.

The large putting green accommodates long and short shots, and provides entertainment for beginners or more advanced players. The artificial turf green and its surrounding fringe blend nicely into the living lawn. The putting green is bordered by large planting areas and a sand trap, which doubles as a sandbox for the grandchildren.

The outdoor dining area is surrounded with citrus trees under-planted with fragrant rosemary and scented geraniums. The bar and barbeque area features a cast concrete countertop embellished with colorful crushed glass polished to a smooth finish. A streambed divides the outdoor areas, and a faux wood bridge provides access between the two spaces. (The stained and stamped concrete was so realistic that when the owner first saw it he called to complain that we used real wood instead of the low-maintenance concrete we'd promised. I told him to go knock on the "wood" and call me back. He did and we had a good chuckle.)

ProjectProfiles

Full Feature Makeover

With children moving into the college years, this outdoor-oriented family was ready for a more grown-up backyard. They wanted to update their tired landscape, remodel their undersized spa, create a space for outdoor entertaining, and design a kitchen suitable for Dad, the home's resident outdoor chef. The wine enthusiast owners also wanted a place to relax and enjoy their hobby.

We created a multi-functional yard to keep the family entertained through the college years, weddings, grandchildren, and beyond.

The new backyard is centered around a 1,000-square-foot pavilion and includes a putting green, basketball court, outdoor kitchen, pool, spa, gazebo, bathroom, and outdoor shower. (ABOVE AND OPPOSITE PAGE)

For the cook who likes to slow-smoke racks of ribs, we added a custom outdoor grill rack in the fireplace. The rack can be lowered for more heat and smoke or raised out of sight when not in use.

The full-featured outdoor kitchen also includes a Teppan grill, full-sized refrigerator, garbage disposal, and dishwasher.

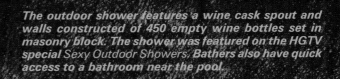

The outdoor shower features a wine cask spout and walls constructed of 450 empty wine bottles set in masonry block. The shower was featured on the HGTV special *Sexy Outdoor Showers*. Bathers also have quick access to a bathroom near the pool.

The barbeque counter sports a custom tile vine mosaic by Michele Griffoul, a ceramic artist friend of mine from Buellton, California. On top, we created a cast concrete countertop embellished with colorful melted wine bottles. Using a special process, we melt the bottles, inset them into the concrete, and polish the counter into one smoothly integrated piece. Fiber optic lighting from below gives the wine bottles a subtle glow after dark.

If you frequently entertain little swimmers, consider bathroom placement. The closer the bathroom is to the pool, the more likely it will actually be used. Also, when possible, preserve existing hardscape to minimize waste. In this project, we used a textured rubberized coating to turn an old abandoned patio into a basketball court and around the pool, we stained and etched the existing concrete to look like flagstone. This produced a softer, more natural look, saved the client thousands of dollars, and minimized the disposal of waste materials.

In a shaded area that was difficult to maintain for a family with active kids and dogs, the artificial turf putting green added entertainment value while solving a number of problems. Meanwhile, a fire pit filled with blue recycled crushed glass provides warmth for bathers relaxing around the spa.

CHAPTER 5

Splash Happy Fun

Swimming pools, water slides, splash decks, & more water fun

Swimming pool design has evolved a lot over the last several years, as the pool is no longer just rectangle-shaped for lap swimming or even simply a place to cool off. Many of today's pools even skip the traditional diving board for safety and liability reasons. Instead, the pools offer a variety of other amenities for sports, recreation, and entertainment.

Pools are also becoming shallower; this makes them easier to maintain and allows for warmer water using less energy. Some pools also feature a sport layout, which is shallow at both ends. This makes them great sites for basketball, volleyball, water polo, and other games. Take caution though: A six- to seven-foot depth is only safe for jumping in feet first. We recommend never diving into a pool headfirst.

When a home includes a swimming pool, it's always the hub of family fun. I was lucky enough to grow up in a home with a pool and some of my fondest memories were made there.

Safe Pool Design

Poolside safety is priority one in design and use. Make sure the deck surface is not too slippery. For maximum traction, we avoid the use of most concrete and stone sealers in the pool area.

Secure fencing is also essential, not only for the safety of your own family but also for visitors and neighborhood kids. Fencing can be constructed of iron, wood, or chain-link, but these types of fences can dominate space and interrupt traffic flow at parties. One option I like is removable mesh fencing like the products offered by Guardian Pool Fence. These stretch securely into place, are unobtrusive, and can easily be taken down for parties.

Adult supervision is another critical element of pool safety, even when the pool is relatively shallow. Accidents don't typically happen when equipment is being used appropriately. It's when your child's classmate decides it would be fun to try skateboarding down the slide or when the group starts piecing bungee cords together to make their own rope swing that trouble happens. It's important for kids to understand the rules and for adults to be there to enforce them.

CAUTION: *When planning a pool party with ten or more kids, consider hiring a lifeguard. This will help ensure safety and give the adults at the party more peace of mind.*

CAUTION: *A pool fence is only effective if you lock it. Don't get casual about keeping it locked. It takes only two minutes for a child to drown.*

Fun Features

Although diving boards may not be an option, a host of new features makes the pool the place to be for active families. Consider one or more of these:

WATER SLIDES | ROPE SWING
SUN SHELF OR "BAJA" SHELF
BEACH ENTRY | DECK JET
SPLASH DECK | BRIDGE
OUTDOOR SHOWER

Slides are becoming much more popular as engineered fiberglass systems are becoming more affordable for the home market. Companies that previously built slides only for water parks are now creating component systems that can be put together to make backyard pool slides in a nearly infinite variety of shapes, sizes, and colors.

Slides can be as simple as a pre-fabricated model purchased from the pool store to a custom slide that twists and turns forty feet down the hillside. They can be open or enclosed and can be designed for use with or without a tube. Most slides can be plumbed to re-circulate pool water up and down the flume. Slides are tested before installation using computer modeling to determine speed, angles, and safety.

DESIGN TIP

For even more excitement, you can create a dark cave-like tunnel with an enclosed tube slide and faux rock.

When you were a kid, remember the thrill of grabbing the rope, launching from the bank, and swinging wide before you dropped into your favorite swimming hole? Some homeowners are bringing that exhilarating feeling to their backyard pool. A rope swing can be installed on a tall structure adjacent to the pool. There are many details to be considered such as weight, swing distance, and load. All can affect safety and fun, so be sure you consult a structural engineer for this custom project.

People may say they want a pool to swim laps and for exercise, but have you ever noticed that what people really like to do in the pool is hang out on the steps? A sun shelf gives everyone a chance to do just that. Also known as a "Baja Shelf" or "Tanning Shelf," it's really a large shallow step that serves as a cool perch for lounge chairs, a safe play area for young children, and a warm spot halfway in and halfway out of the water. It's the perfect place for reading your Kindle or enjoying a cocktail with friends. Allow at least six to eight feet of width for lounge chairs and twelve to eighteen inches of water depth. Consider including an umbrella stand for those hot days.

A pop-up fountain adds refreshing fun to a Baja Shelf. These pop up with a decorative spray pattern that kids love to run through. When not in use, they drop down flush to the pool floor. Choose from "Foaming Cascade" or "Shower of Diamonds" patterns.

Like a sun shelf, this is another way to offer a gradual entry into the pool. Instead of a step down, it offers a very slight slope into the water. It works especially well for a tropical themed pool or for those who want to mimic a natural beach. However, a beach entry takes up quite a bit more space than a sun shelf and will cause more water to splash out. Many sunbathers also find the angle less comfortable than the level platform of a sun shelf.

Everyone likes to play under the hose on a hot day. A deck jet is a small fountain that shoots from the deck surface into the pool. For just a little extra cost, one or more deck jets add a lot of motion, sound, and entertainment value to a pool. They're lots of fun to swim under and jets are available in various sizes and spray patterns.

Often seen at water parks and other recreation spots, a splash deck features eight to ten deck jets that spray water into the air often in short, surprising bursts or spray patterns. They can emerge from a shallow sun shelf or from a deck adjacent to the pool. For more drama, these can be tied into a lighting system with fiber optics or LED lights and programmed to shoot in various whimsical arrays. (Think Bellagio in your backyard!)

A small footbridge across a section of the pool is another way to integrate architectural beauty to the waterscape. It also makes a perfect jumping off point. A bridge can provide an inviting transition from pool deck to patio or even solve an awkward spacing problem. It can be constructed with concrete and colored and stamped to complement just about any theme or decor. Be sure to allow adequate clearance underneath for swimmers (a minimum of eighteen inches from water surface to bridge), and enough depth for a comfortable jump into the water.

WATER SLIDES | ROPE SWING
SUN SHELF OR "BAJA" SHELF
BEACH ENTRY | DECK JET
SPLASH DECK | BRIDGE
OUTDOOR SHOWER

An alfresco shower can be fun for the whole family (perhaps one at a time) and it's a great way to enhance your backyard theme with another design element. Consider adding privacy walls. These also serve as a great canvas for decorative details. The pool equipment screen wall is a natural place for an outdoor shower.

Blue Lagoon

A tropical lagoon is the highlight of this backyard designed for kid-friendly action, lively entertainment, and adult relaxation.

A naturalistic waterfall spills over rocks into an inviting spa. With heated water, the cascade provides a therapeutic shoulder massage. Jungle plantings surround the free-form pool and spa, providing an intimate retreat within this residential neighborhood. Faux boulders create a stepped entry into the water and an inviting climbing wall for kids. A ladder up the "cliff" leads to a hidden waterslide and a faux-wood concrete foot bridge adds to the Swiss Family Robinson appeal. Courtesy of Paul Jonason.

When they're not in the pool, family and guests can play on the full-size bocce court or on the lawn, which was sized for Blongo Ball, volleyball, croquet, and other games. A vine-covered wrought iron pergola provides color and shade over the bocce court.

Adjacent to the pool, a twelve-foot Tiki bar and outdoor kitchen offers convenient access to dinner, snacks, and beverages. Tiki torches, a cozy fire-pit, outdoor lighting, and a sound system keep the party going into the night. A cast concrete countertop embedded with crushed glass and lit with fiber optics adds a splash of whimsical color after dark.

Backyard Adventure

This homeowner wanted a child-friendly yard with something for everyone from preschoolers to teens to adults. The main attraction is the sunny, quarry-style pool and water slide.

To maximize space in this project, we turned the side yard into a play area where the younger set can hopscotch or play in the sandbox. A hands-on mother/daughter project resulted in the pretty tiles in the hopscotch path; hand-decorated tiles, hand-painted designs, stamped concrete, and other personal and artistic touches give families an opportunity to make memories that last beyond childhood.

This play yard also does double duty as an out-of-the-way place to stash all the big outdoor toys when company comes.

▼ *Swimmers climb the footpath up the steep hillside before descending the slide's twisting 52-foot-long flume.*

▲ The rear bond beam of the pool makes an irresistible jumping off point for splash-happy kids (and adults).

◀ Raising the spa allowed us to create a swim-up bar for quick access to juice or cocktails. A generously sized Baja shelf and patio provide comfortable spots for adults to lounge while supervising the kids.

For the best cannonball launching pad, provide a jumping off point about three feet above water level. For safety, be sure the water here is at least seven feet deep and strictly enforce the "no diving" rule.

Spanish Style Resort

Entertaining is a way of life for these homeowners. They wanted a backyard resort where they could host large groups in style. To anchor the space we created a large pavilion that partially shades the pool. It houses a recessed outdoor kitchen, dance floor, restroom, and changing area.

The pool features a sport layout; shallow sides on each end make it easy to play volleyball, basketball, and other pool games. A mist system cools the yard.

We also turned this side yard into a children's play area. Two kissing topiary giraffes provide a whimsical entrance to the area, which features a hopscotch path, sandbox, and play set. On "dive-in movie" nights, two large outdoor TVs allow kids to enjoy the view from a raft in the pool or spa.

Photo by Paul Jonason.

Photo by Paul Jonason.

Hacienda de la Fiesta

After enjoying quite a few rides on a rope swing at a resort hotel pool in Hawaii, these homeowners wanted to recreate that thrill at home. A tropical theme was their original plan, but we knew we could offer the same experience in a style more in keeping with the home's Spanish Mediterranean architecture. With full artistic license from the client, we created this multi-featured Spanish mission style yard.

The highlight is an eighteen-foot-tall bell tower and rope swing. The twenty-foot-wide pool allows riders to sail wide over the water before dropping in. A climb up the hillside steps leads to a resort style waterslide with a 45-foot-long flume. According to family rumor, the fastest way down the slide is without a swimsuit. (Sorry, no photographic evidence is available.)
(ABOVE AND OPPOSITE PAGE)

CAUTION: *Rope swings are not a do-it-yourself project. Any structure designed to hold human weight requires the expertise of a structural engineer. And remember, rope swings and waterslides always require rules and adult supervision.*

To continue the resort theme, the yard includes a bocce ball court and a half-court basketball surface marked with rubberized coating. The subdued palette ensures that the basketball court doesn't compete with the rest of the décor.

A split level barbeque counter accommodates comfortable cooking and bar height dining with space for eight barstools. A 1,000-square-foot covered patio in materials that match the home completes this backyard.

A Baja shelf flanked by two fire bowls generously accommodates loungers. The raised spa allows for a swim-up bar and provides a great spot for a water feature. Between the pool and spa, water spills over colorful mosaic tile.

Cascade Falls

The sights and sounds of moving water are featured throughout this backyard. Water cascades into the pool over a series of naturalistic faux rock falls as a 25-foot-long slide runs alongside. Overhanging rocks create a cozy spot big enough for swimmers to enjoy the view from inside the grotto (and maybe even sneak a kiss behind the waterfall).

▲ A foot bridge leads over the pool to the pavilion. Bridges like this help maximize space while adding architectural interest.

▼ Slopes can be difficult to work with, but we took advantage of the slope here by creating a raised spa and adjacent fire pit with a built-in seat wall.

With excellent sun exposure, this home was a great candidate for a solar pool heating system. This captures green energy as water circulates through roof-top tubes on its way to the pool and spa. Note: A growing number of homeowners are discovering solar roof systems as a greener option for heating the pool and extending a swim season. Timers allow the spa to be warm and ready when you get home from work. If you have a homeowner's association, be sure to check guidelines. Some require that solar systems not be visible from the street.

Water continues in the side yard with a pondless waterfall. This advancement in pond design is a safe choice for families with young children. Instead of emptying into a pond, the water flows into a collection basin and re-circulates back to the top of the falls.

An outdoor shower is accented with dark blue tiles to match the pool.

A cast concrete countertop features colorful embedded glass lit from below with fiber optic lighting.

To keep the kids busy when they're not in the pool, we added a 30"-wide concrete riding path that snakes around the yard. Striped to look like a road with reflective paint, it gives kids a safe place to race along on their Big Wheels, bikes, tricycles, and scooters. The path separates the lawn from planting beds and offers a comfortable place to stroll through the garden.

Entertaining with Ease

Welcoming Guests of All Ages

One of the biggest rewards of creating a backyard built for fun is sharing it with family and friends. Neighborhood barbeques, children's parties, family reunions, and even business get-togethers all take on a little more magic when they're held outdoors.

However, successful outdoor entertaining isn't just about impressing the neighbors, the boss, or the in-laws with your amazing backyard. It's about setting the stage for fun to happen spontaneously. It means understanding your guests and knowing what makes them feel welcomed and special. Most importantly a successful backyard party is one where you can actually relax and enjoy the festivities yourself instead of worrying about all the details.

It starts with a thoughtful entertainment plan and a well-designed outdoor space. Consider the following:

How often will you entertain?

Do you live in a neighborhood where everyone takes turns hosting the next big party? Does your work require regular entertaining? Do you have years of children's birthday parties ahead of you? If so, take your entertaining needs seriously when you're planning your backyard. You'll thank yourself over and over during every future party.

How big are your get-togethers?

Are we talking quiet dinner parties for one or two other couples? Or do you regularly host large crowds? Depending on the frequency of your parties, create a plan for both.

The party set?

Is your backyard arrangement for a bigger bash? It may mean using the basketball court as a dance floor, pulling out some folding tables, converting the pool table to a dining set, and making space for a bartender or caterer. Even if you don't hold major events often, a plan for how it will all come together when you do will make your entertaining much easier.

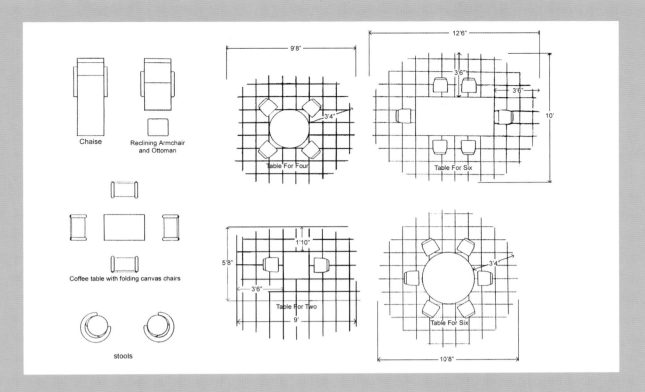

Chaise

Reclining Armchair and Ottoman

Coffee table with folding canvas chairs

stools

9'8"

3'4"

Table For Four

12'6"

3'6"

3'6"

10'

Table For Six

1'10"

5'8"

3'6"

9'

Table For Two

3'4"

Table For Six

10'8"

The everyday backyard layout should accommodate family dining and simple entertaining. You'll want to include comfortable seating and dining space for the whole family and a few guests.

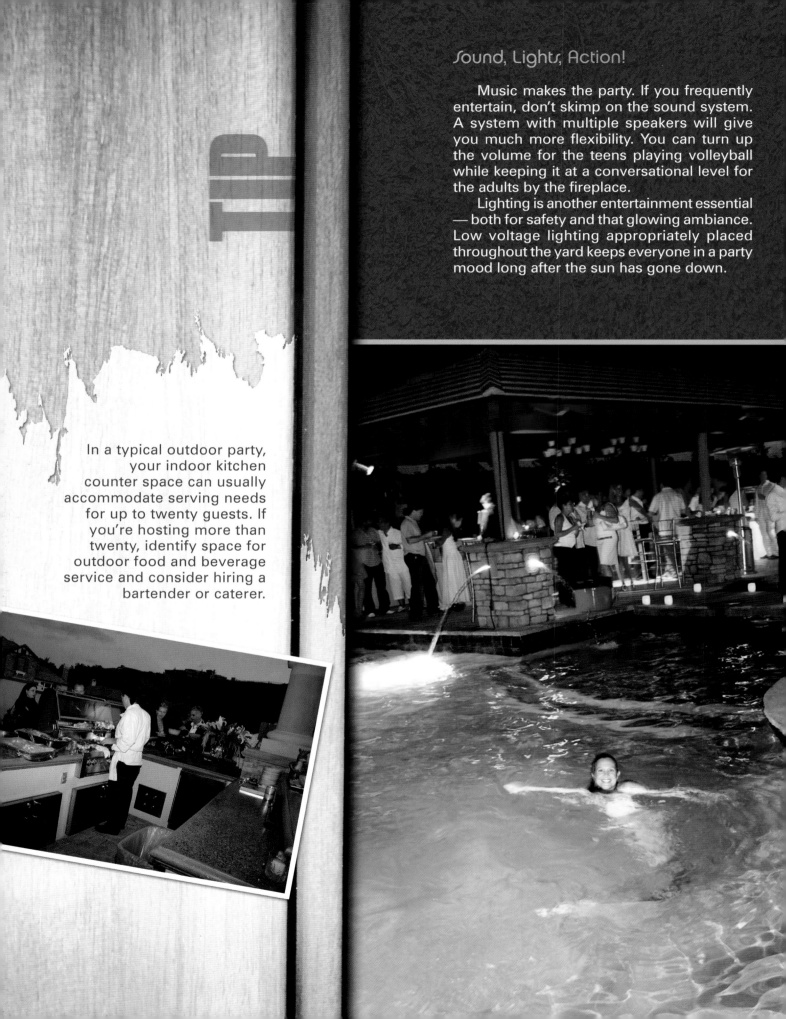

Sound, Lights, Action!

Music makes the party. If you frequently entertain, don't skimp on the sound system. A system with multiple speakers will give you much more flexibility. You can turn up the volume for the teens playing volleyball while keeping it at a conversational level for the adults by the fireplace.

Lighting is another entertainment essential — both for safety and that glowing ambiance. Low voltage lighting appropriately placed throughout the yard keeps everyone in a party mood long after the sun has gone down.

TIP

In a typical outdoor party, your indoor kitchen counter space can usually accommodate serving needs for up to twenty guests. If you're hosting more than twenty, identify space for outdoor food and beverage service and consider hiring a bartender or caterer.

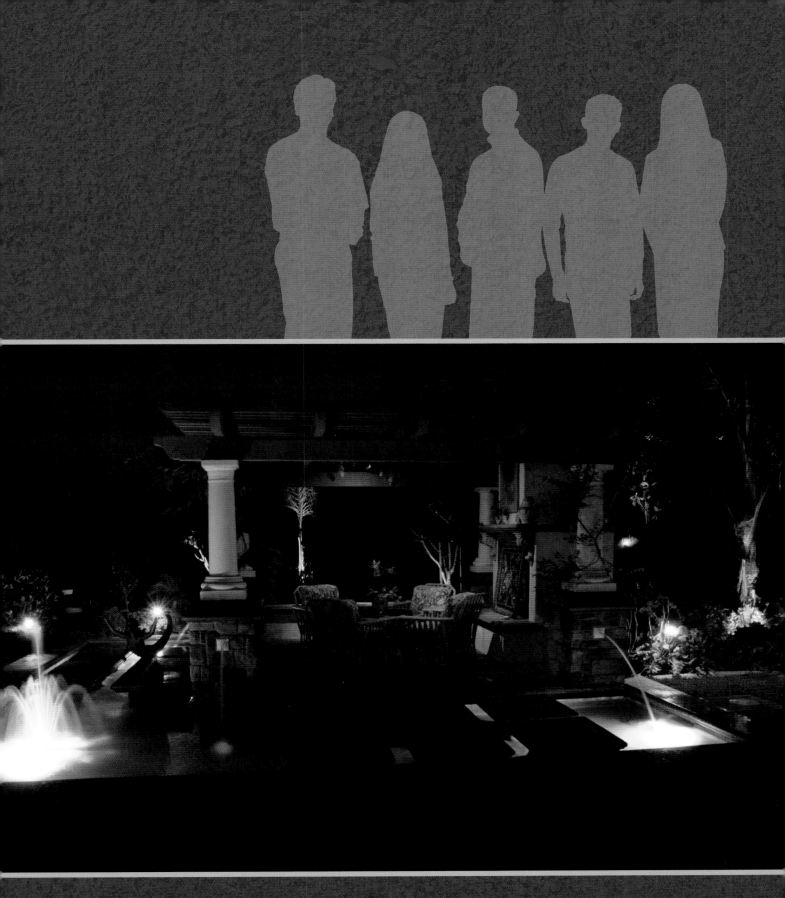

Nothing adds warmth or sparks conversation more than a backyard fire. Decide whether you want a fireplace, a fire pit, or both. An upright fireplace presents a more sophisticated architectural statement and creates a space conducive to quiet conversation for couples or small groups. A fire pit can be an intimate setting, but with its 360-degree seating, it is also a natural gathering spot for groups of all ages. It calls out for stories, jokes, and, of course, s'mores.

Dive-In Movies

Backyard movies are a growing highlight at family parties, thanks in part to TV sets designed for outdoor use. Sets like the ones manufactured by SunBrightTV can be kept outside and won't be damaged by rain or other elements. As prices drop, they've become increasingly popular in the residential market.

Be sure to choose a television large enough to accommodate your typical viewing distance. (Measure; don't guess. Then follow manufacturers' recommendations). Avoid placing TVs where they'll be in the glare of the sun during prime viewing hours. Better yet, mount the TV on an articulating arm that can be adjusted for different viewing angles throughout the day. You can watch the game from the outdoor kitchen while you're at the grill and then spin the TV around so the kids can watch their movie from the pool.

Another option is to rent a large inflatable projector screen. Just like an inflatable bouncer, the company you rent from sets it up, plays the movie, and takes it down afterwards. However, if backyard movies will only be an occasional event, a digital projector is a less expensive option. Use a portable screen or simply set up a white sheet. For the best picture, wait until it's really dark.

TIP

Lay out your party plan before you do any building. Measure your space and make templates using paper, magnets, sticky notes, or the computer to illustrate how the tables, chairs, bartender, caterer, and other elements will fit for both everyday dining and major parties. Think about where people will mingle, how they'll move from space to space, even where they'll set down their beverages. This level of planning may seem picky now but it will help you avoid that "if only…" feeling down the road.

A lawn area with built-in seat walls offers extra seating for guests of all ages and works great as a mini-theater.

Children's Entertainment

If your backyard will see lots of birthday parties, bar/bat and mitzvahs, quinceañeras, graduation parties, and other children's events, think ahead: Where will the magician, the juggler, the DJ, or the balloon animal guy set up the show? What about the piñata?

While you don't need a dedicated area just for parties, allowing enough space somewhere in the yard for the entertainer and children's games means fewer details to worry about on party day. Also, children's entertainers often use music as part of the act. If you're including a sound system in your yard and you're planning to host children's events, consider placing speakers in the kid zone.

Concrete Seat Walls

Well placed seat walls are a simple and low cost way to incorporate a focal point that serves as an entertaining area, as well as a showcase for design materials, such as natural stone, into any outdoor garden space.

When designing outdoor space for entertaining, one of the first things I do is divide the space into outdoor rooms. One terrific way to create the feeling of different rooms or spaces is to create varying levels in the yards.

I accomplish this by using a series of cast concrete steps and low retaining walls designed at seat height. The placement of seat walls in the garden can create great focal points. Use these low, unobtrusive walls to surround and highlight a fountain or favorite water feature, create a raised tree planter, or add substantial seating area for entertaining guests.

How to Add Seating in an Outdoor Room

In large gardens, seat walls help define outdoor rooms, identify space, and highlight focal points. Seat walls add sitting room for entertaining without taking up much room. The use of well-placed seat walls can easily add seating for ten to fifteen guests.

Plan on 22–24" of width for each "seat" you expect to accommodate on the wall. As outdoor furniture continues to rise in cost, built-in seating can add great value to your project.

Seat Wall Construction Tips

Construction of seat walls is easy and does not require any special permits in most communities. A typical seat wall is constructed using 8–12" wide cinder block and topping it with a decorative cap of brick, stone, or bull-nosed cast concrete. If you use stone, be sure to soften sharp edges that might cut into the backs of legs. Use a grinder to hone edges and create a smoother surface.

Industry standard for adult seating height is 18–22" tall, with a seat depth of 12–18", perfect for a low, easy-to-build masonry wall. Walls should be shorter to accommodate small children. Use these guidelines to assist with your layout:

Child's Age (YEARS)	Seat Height
1 to 4	10–12"
5 to 7	12–14"
8 to 10	13–17"
11 to 13	15–18"

Be sure and provide adequate drainage and waterproof your seat walls when using them as planters or small retaining walls. Proper waterproofing will reduce unsightly mineral buildup on the face of the walls caused by moisture that wicks through from behind. Mineral buildup can ruin the look of your walls and create a maintenance nightmare for your clients. The addition of "French" style hydrostatic relief drains or even simple weep holes will relieve water pressure from behind walls.

Pirates' Booty

A true backyard fantasy, this Robinson Crusoe-themed pool practically guarantees imaginative, active fun for family and guests. Trapped on a desert island, there's really nothing else to do but play.

The spa is a faux-wood boat run aground on the rocks and inundated with water. A leak in the hull sprays water into the free-form tropical pool. A faux-wood concrete dock and a 25-foot slide with a hidden cave underneath keep the adventure alive.

Luckily for the castaways, this desert island also happens to have a putting green. The sand-trap serves as both a beach and sandbox. When the guests are gone and the kids are in bed, the yard becomes a romantic tropical escape for parents.

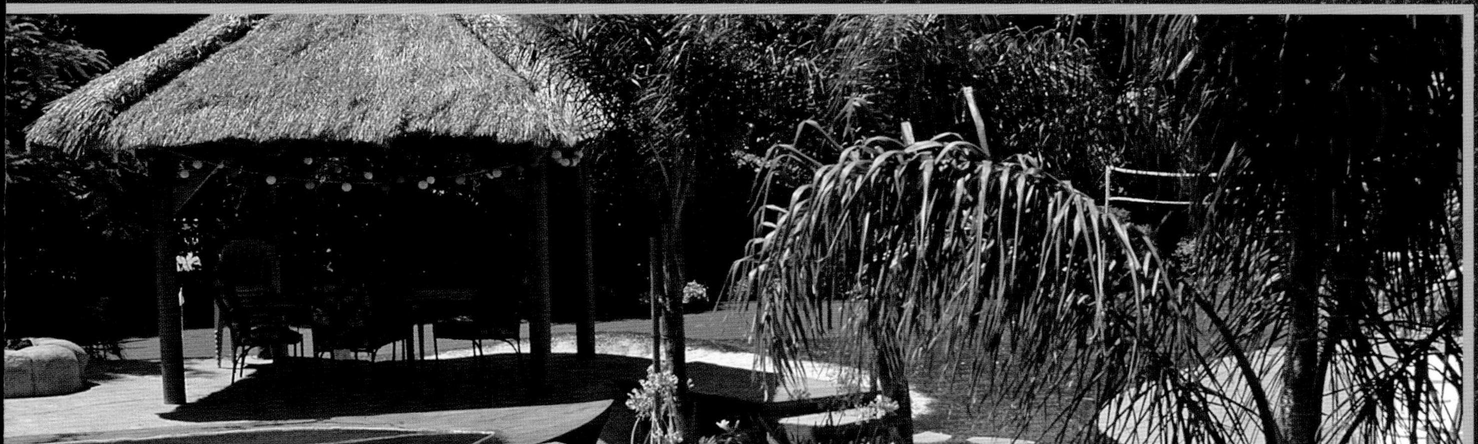

CHAPTER 6 Entertaining with Ease

Tropical Water Park

With a large family of kids, ages eight to eighteen, this home is a constant hub of activity for neighbors, friends, and visiting cousins. The owners dreamed of a resort-style backyard and were willing to wait a few years until they had the funds needed to make it happen.

The result was worth the wait. We gave them a tropical backyard water park with a generously sized pool and spa and a 65-foot-long water slide. The pool and spa area features boulders for climbing up and jumping in, a swim-up bar, and a series of waterfalls, including one in the spa that provides a hot, soothing shoulder massage. Another waterfall spills over a whimsical toucan tile mosaic by Michelle Griffoul Studios. A concrete path with dinosaur "fossils" leads the way to the slide. A fire pit and seat walls adjacent to the spa keep everyone toasty and together on cool nights.

The yard also includes a 400-square-foot Palapa, which houses an outdoor kitchen. The counter, which seats twelve, sports another Griffoul mosaic. Cooling misters, Tiki torches, and an extensive outdoor sound system complete this entertainment-oriented backyard playground.

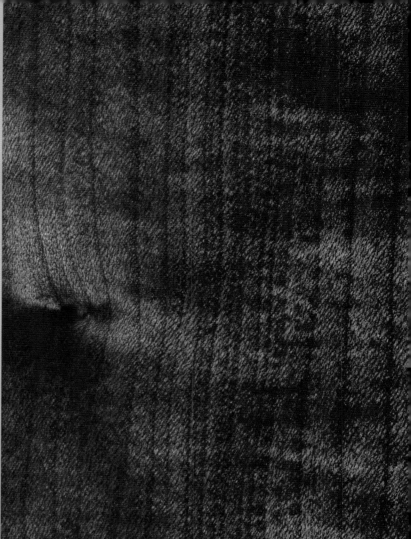

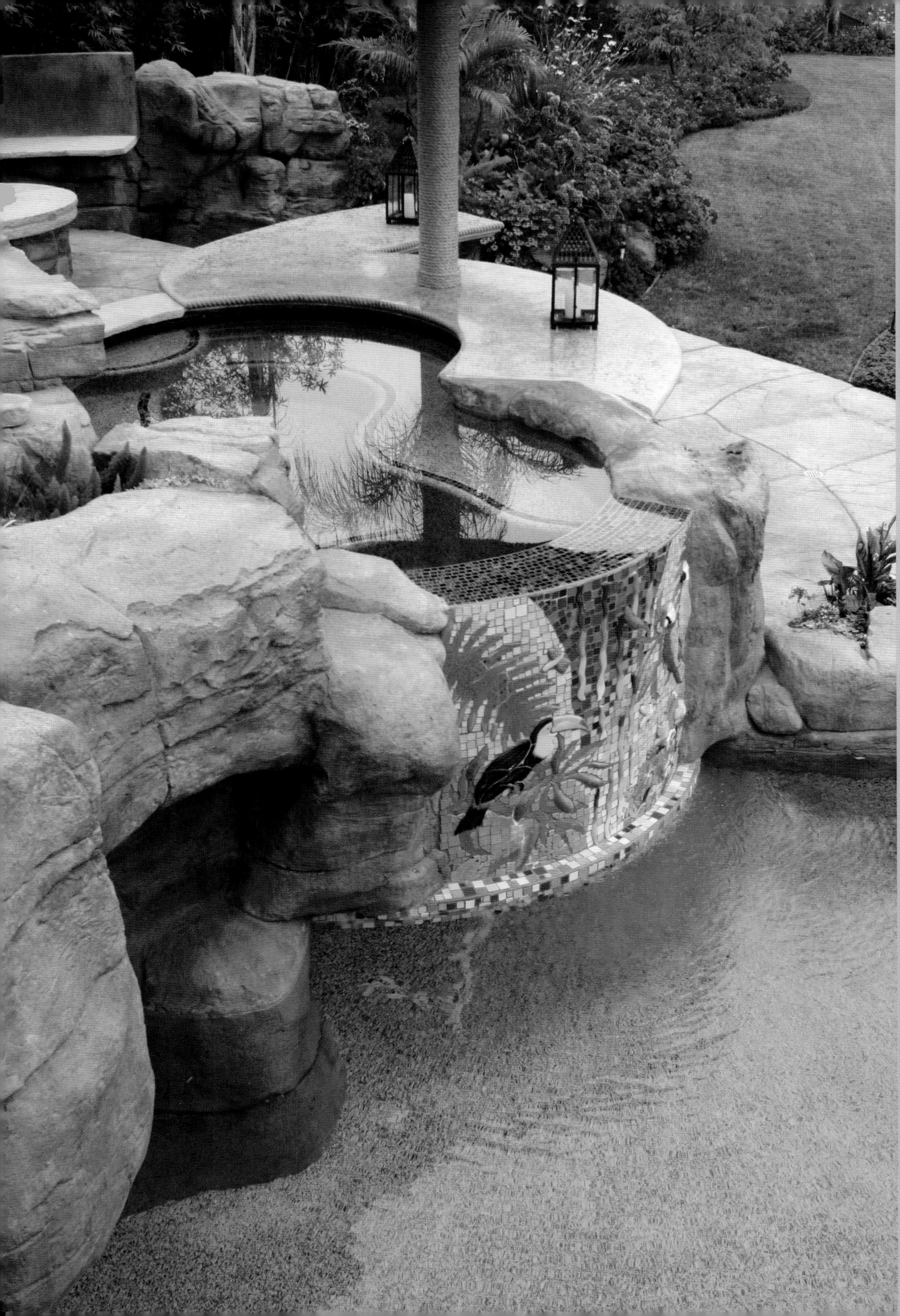

CHAPTER 6 Entertaining with Ease

Afterword

I hope you will have as much fun implementing the ideas in this book as I did putting them all together! We would love to hear from you and see the before and after pictures of your projects! Please share your stories and photos with us at our website www.FamilyFunBackyards.com.

From my family to yours, we wish your yard and garden truly becomes "the place to be" and remember: A family that plays together, stays together!

Scott Cohen

This image is of my three daughters when they were active in the YMCA Indian Guides program. This parent-child program creates a fantastic opportunity to bond with your kids and help them grow to be confident leaders.